COVENANT • BIBLE • STUDIES

Ephesians
Reconciled in Christ

Donna Ritchey Martin

faithQuest ◆ Brethren Press

Unless otherwise noted, scripture quotations are from the New Revised Standard Version of the Bible, copyrighted 1989 by the National Council of Churches of Christ in the USA, Division of Education and Ministry.

Cover photo by Don Ford

98 97 96 95 94   5 4 3 2 1

Library of Congress Cataloging-in-Publication Data

Martin, Donna Ritchey.
　　Ephesians / Donna Ritchey Martin.
　　　　p.　　cm. — (Covenant Bible study series)
　　ISBN 0-87178-221-9 (pbk.)
　　　　1. Bible. N.T. Ephesians—Study and teaching. I. Title. II. Series.
BS2695.5.M37 1994
227'.5'007—dc20   94-11717

Manufactured in the United States of America

Contents

Foreword

The Covenant Bible Study Series was first developed for a denominational program in the Church of the Brethren and the Christian Church (Disciples of Christ). This program, called People of the Covenant, was founded on the concept of relational Bible study and has been adopted by several other denominations and small groups who want to study the Bible in a community rather than alone.

Relational Bible study is marked by certain characteristics, some of which differ from other types of Bible study. For one, it is intended for small groups of people who can meet face-to-face on a regular basis and share frankly with an intimate group.

It is important to remember that relational Bible study is anchored in covenantal history. God covenanted with people in Old Testament history, established a new covenant in Jesus Christ, and covenants with the church today.

Relational Bible study takes seriously a corporate faith. As each person contributes to study, prayer, and work, the group becomes the real body of Christ. Each one's contribution is needed and important. "For just as the body is one and has many members, and all the members of the body, though many, are one body, so it is with Christ. . . . Now you are the body of Christ and individually members of it" (1 Cor. 12:12, 17).

Relational Bible study helps both individuals and the group to claim the promise of the Spirit and the working of the Spirit. As one person testified, "In our commitment to one another and in our sharing, something happened. . . . We were woven together in love by the master Weaver. It is something that can happen only when two or three or seven are gathered in God's name, and we know the promise of God's presence in our lives."

The symbol for these covenant Bible study groups is the burlap cross. The interwoven threads, the uniqueness of each strand, the unrefined fabric, and the rough texture characterize covenant groups. The people in the groups are unique but interrelated; they are imperfect and unpolished, but loving and supportive.

The shape that these divergent threads create is the cross, the symbol for all Christians of the resurrection and presence with us of Christ our Savior. Like the burlap cross, we are brought together, simple and ordinary, to be sent out again in all directions to be in the world.

For people who choose to use this study in a small group, the following guidelines will help create an atmosphere in which support will grow and faith will deepen.

1. As a small group of learners, we gather around God's word to discern its meaning for today.
2. The words, stories, and admonitions we find in scripture come alive for today, challenging and renewing us.
3. All people are learners and all are leaders.
4. Each person will contribute to the study, sharing the meaning found in the scripture and helping to bring meaning to others.
5. We recognize each other's vulnerability as we share out of our own experience, and in sharing we learn to trust others and to be trustworthy.

Additional suggestions for study and group-building are provided in the "Sharing and Prayer" section. They are intended for use in the hour preceding the Bible study to foster intimacy in the covenant group and relate personal sharing to the Bible study topic.

Welcome to this study. As you search the scriptures, may you also search yourself. May God's voice and guidance and the love and encouragement of brothers and sisters in Christ challenge you to live more fully the abundant life God promises.

Preface

To catch the vision of Ephesians is to change the way we look at the world. For Ephesians sees all of creation from God's point of view. In a world of strife and disunity, Ephesians shows us Christ, in whom there is reconciliation and unity and in whose body each believer has an important place.

The material in this short letter is incredibly rich. Much of it is familiar. The great theological themes of scripture are all here. Chapters 1—3 sing about God's plan of salvation in Christ Jesus for the whole world. Chapters 4—6 give instructions for the believers who want their lives to reflect God's plan.

In the limited space of these pages, we can focus on only a few of the great themes of Ephesians. I hope these lessons will be a starting point for each individual and each group to study further and to begin looking at our world and our lives through God's loving, grace-filled eyes.

Donna Ritchey Martin

Recommended Resources:

Foster, Richard J. *Celebration of Discipline.* Harper and Row, 1988.
James, Ron. *Jesus Christ in Ephesians.* The Upper Room, 1988.

1

God's Great Plan
Ephesians 1:3-23

Paul sings a song of praise for God's plan of salvation and for the blessings bestowed on the believers. He offers a prayer of thanksgiving for the readers and for God's power at work in Christ.

Personal Preparation

1. Read Ephesians 1:3-23. What is our inheritance as Christians? Think about what you would do with a large inheritance. In what ways would you feel compelled to honor the memory of your benefactor? In what ways would you like to use the money for yourself?
2. In Ephesians, Paul tells us of God's desire for unity. In what ways does your congregation or small group bring unity? What areas of church life need more unity? What suggestions do you have for unity in the church, in families, and in the world?

Understanding

I am not an artist. Although I enjoy the artistic expressions of others, my creativity goes into more practical things, such as making quilts and filling quart jars with garden vegetables and writing Bible study lessons. But, friends, we are about to begin studying art. When we read the Letter to the Ephesians we are not reading a textbook, but a well-written letter to young churches, with snatches of hymns and long flowery lines of the poetry of praise and worship of God. This is the language of poem and song, rich in metaphor and symbolic imagery, a treasure trove of devotional literature by a true artist.

Serious students of Ephesians quickly encounter some very real problems with the book. Scholars point out that there are good grounds for questioning whether the apostle Paul authored the Letter to the Ephesians. For our purposes, we will accept the traditional view that the author of Ephesians is "Paul, a prisoner for Christ Jesus" (3:1). We can imagine Paul writing from prison in Rome very near the end of his life. Scholars also question whether this letter was originally addressed to a single congregation in the city of Ephesus, since the words "in Ephesus" (1:1) do not appear in all the ancient manuscripts of the New Testament. (Some Bibles have a note about this.) For our purposes, we will assume that the author intended this letter to be read in the congregations around Ephesus.

We will study the text as the church has preserved it for us. We will study Ephesians as a literary whole, on its own, within its own limits. We will listen for the special messages of Ephesians and for the letter's unique ways of talking about God, Christ, the church, and faithful living. I hope you discover some surprises along the way. I have.

Today's lesson is based on only two sentences, but they are *long* sentences. In the Greek text, verses 3-14 and verses 15-23 are both monstrous, run-on sentences. Paul added phrase upon phrase as if he couldn't bear to stop. Later, translators divided the two sentences into shorter units to make them easier to understand.

Verses 3-14 are a song of praise to God. The opening words "Blessed be . . . God" can also be translated "Praise be to God" or "Let us give thanks to God." Each phrase that follows gives a reason for singing praises. Paul lists gift after gift and blessing after blessing, all of which God has accomplished through Christ on our behalf. When we let the words wash over us, we can only shake our heads in amazement, as in the words of the hymn, "lost in wonder, love and praise."

It is tempting to pull apart these verses for study. We will have to do some of that. But Paul sang this song "all in one breath," wrote it all in one sentence for a reason. He's singing about God's plan for unity of all creation. He's singing about God's grace, action, and revelation. He's singing about God the Creator, Christ the Redeemer, and about the Holy Spirit who is the Guarantor for all God's promises. All the pieces fit together. If we dissect too much, we will be left with only pieces instead of the grand unity Paul wants us to appreciate and appropriate.

Having said that, here is one plan for organizing verses 3-14:

> Let us praise God
> who, through Christ, (v. 3)
> chose to adopt us as God's children, (vv. 4-6)
> redeemed and forgave us, (vv. 7-8)
> showed us the divine plan to unite ALL things
>   (even Jews and Gentiles). (vv. 9-14)

Seen simply, the "spiritual blessings" mentioned in 1:3 are neither otherworldly nor abstract. They are promises for and changes in the flesh-and-blood people of the church.

When I started studying for these lessons, I used Ephesians for Bible study sessions at the nursing home down the street. Only a very few of those who attended were able to participate in a discussion. They were in poor health and largely forgotten by others, indeed "the least of these." But tired eyes lit up as folks heard that they were precious, chosen children of God, part of God's plan. Their eager response was surely the kind of praise that Paul had hoped to inspire.

In 1:15-23, Paul continues to radiate his joy in a prayer of thanksgiving. Once again it is easier to describe the various themes and subdivisions of this sentence than to explain why they are coherent. But certainly Paul wanted to hold them all together. The flow of the prayer begins with thanksgiving for the faithfulness of Paul's readers and then proceeds to intercession for the gifts of the Spirit, who reveals the hope, the riches, and the power given by God. Then Paul describes God's power to both resurrect and exalt Christ. He concludes where he started, with the church, which he describes as the very body of Christ.

Ephesians says, "Have I got a plan for you!" The drama of God's plan for human history began before creation. In creation, God made the world and declared it good. In the life and death of Jesus of Nazareth, God's plan came into focus. In the resurrection, God clearly demonstrated the power by which the divine drama is being carried out. Paul wants the church to know that it is part of God's plan of salvation and unity for all creation. Paul does not try to prove or explain God's plan and Christ's purpose in it. He assumes both and celebrates them.

There are two main actors in God's drama: Christ and the church. Verses 20-23 contain one of the strongest statements of Christ's authority in the New Testament. Christ is Lord and Savior not only of individual lives, but of the whole universe. His authority extends over the "principalities and powers," that is, the institutions and structures of society and any other powers that exercise themselves in the world. Over everything imaginable, Christ is Lord.

The church is the means through which God's plan for the world is to be carried out. The church is the place where Christ's sovereign rule can be seen most clearly. The term *church* in Ephesians does not refer only to a local congregation. The church is not just an organization formed in response to social or even spiritual needs. The church is part of God's plan for "the fullness of time." The church was included in the first draft of God's script before "the foundation of the world."

I look up from my writing and wonder what all this has to do with a troubled modern world, our struggling congregation, and my harried life. The words of Paul's letter sound so fine, but I don't have a plan for supper yet, let alone an understanding of a divine plan for the universe.

I suppose that is why Paul offered such a fervent prayer that his readers might receive a spirit of wisdom and knowledge and hope and a sense of God's power for their lives. As stated earlier, Ephesians is not a textbook, not a how-to explanation. This first chapter, especially, is a song. And in the music we can hear an invitation to find our place in God's plan, to take the stage in God's drama.

Discussion and Action

1. Have someone read aloud Ephesians 1:3-14 and then 1:15-23. Let the words flow over you without having to try to understand each one.

2. Ask questions of one another about the meaning of unclear words and phrases. You may want to try to diagram each of the long sentences, perhaps not as a grammar teacher would but in some way that makes the text easier for you to comprehend.

3. Recall a time when you knew you had been chosen (for a softball team, marriage, a job). Recall a time when you chose someone. Reflect on what it means to you to be chosen by God.

4. Discuss how you do or do not see God's plan at work in the world today. How is Christ's lordship expressed today? What does it mean for you to say "Christ is Lord"?

5. Pay attention to the news this week. Watch TV and read newspapers through the eyes of the Letter to the Ephesians. Look for evidence of God's plan to unite all things in Christ and for expressions of Christ's authority. Where do you see God at work in the world?

6. Bring in news clippings next week about events for which you are grateful and events for which you want your group to pray.

2

Amazing Grace
Ephesians 2:1-10

The text reflects our experience of spiritual death and announces the miracle that God is in the business of granting new life.

Personal Preparation

1. As you read Ephesians 2:1-10, recall the first time the truth of God's amazing grace became real for you.
2. Bring to the group meeting something you have made, an example of your handiwork.

Understanding

The key to this lesson is found right in the middle of the unit, verses 4-6. "But God . . . made us alive together with Christ . . . and raised us up with him . . ." (2:4-6). These verses paint a picture of salvation that differs from the one with which we are most familiar. Instead of salvation as forgiveness of sins, Ephesians 2:1-10 describes salvation as the granting of life to those who are dead. The second chapter of Ephesians describes the "immeasurable greatness of [God's] power" (1:19) in terms of the resurrection not only of Christ but also of the believers.

Paul refers to death in these verses. But does he mean physical death? Here, death is walking the way of "trespasses and sins" (2:1). The Greek word *paraptoma*, translated "trespasses," literally means a slip or a fall. It is used for someone who slips up and takes the wrong turn in a road. The Greek word *hamartia*, usually translated "sins," comes from the archery range. It means a miss, a failure to hit the target. In the New Testament, the term usually refers to a person's failure to hit the mark established by God, that is, to be less than what one was created to be and to be estranged from the source of all life.

Death in this passage is to be controlled by the "power of the air" and the "passions of our flesh" (2:2-3). Many first-century religions believed in a demonic ruler of the earth who lived in the atmosphere. To be spiritually governed by such a false sovereign is to be "dead." We are also dead if our lives are controlled by "the flesh." The flesh itself is not evil. The Bible knows that flesh was created by God as "very good" (Gen. 1:31) and celebrates that Christ came "in the flesh." "The passions of our flesh" refers to the wickedness that lies in us and controls us from within. It is life that is subject only to our own desires and impulses. Traditionally, the church has listed seven deadly sins: anger, gluttony, envy, sloth, avarice, lust, and pride. These are all "passions of our flesh."

So, to be dead is to be living short of the mark God wants for people. To be dead is to be controlled by external influences or internal forces rather than by the Creator.

When have you experienced this kind of death? When did you last experience the human condition described by Clarence Jordan in his paraphrase of Ephesians 2?

> In days gone by you all were living in your sin and filth
> like a bunch of stinking corpses, giving your allegiance
> to material things and ruled by the power of custom.
> (*The Cotton Patch Version of Paul's Epistles* 106)

Some commentators talk about this as "spiritual death," as if this form of death is not as real as physical death. However, for the Bible tradition, death that cuts us off from God and delivers us to the powers of evil is at least as real as, and certainly more dreadful than, physical death. Indeed, today we see the results of such deep alienation and despair in rising suicide rates. For some, physical death seems to be the only answer to the agony of spiritual death.

These opening verses paint the picture of humanity utterly separated from God. These "children of wrath" deserved God's righteous judgment. Then comes verse 4: "BUT GOD" explodes into this hopeless picture. Once again, God creates light out of darkness, order out of chaos, life out of death.

Let us say that spiritual death means at least these four things: (1) alienation from God, (2) broken relationships among people, (3) perversion of the freedom God gives, (4) disintegration of the ability to make wise judgments. To be made alive (2:5) would involve: (1) reconciliation with God, (2) healing of relationships, (3) the ability to receive and use freedom responsibly, (4) the gift of discernment.

When have you been "made alive"? When have you been rescued from the powers and pressures of daily living and given God's perspective and insight and strength? When have you been saved from just going through the motions and given joy and faith instead? When have you been rescued from a controlling addiction and received your life back?

Ephesians 2:4 shifts the focus from the power of God to the love and mercy and grace behind that power. In verses 4-10, Paul is singing again—the song of one who has been given new life, who has been put on the right road, and who has been aimed toward the center of the target.

It is almost too much to believe—that the Creator of the Universe would step into history not to "shape us up," but to love, save, and redeem us. And to do all that simply to "show the immeasurable riches of [God's] grace"!

Once again, God's power and mercy are focused in Christ. We probably have some sense of new life in Christ and even of resurrection. But what does Paul mean when he says that God has "raised us up with him and seated us with him in the heavenly places in Christ Jesus" (2:6)? What is this life of sitting on a throne in heaven? This image points to the *substance* of the new life God has given. Resurrection from the dead does not mean we are simply restored to our previous existence. To receive the grace of new life is to be given a place in God's household, to have a seat at the table with Christ and all the saints. To be raised to the heavenly places is to be given honor and dignity and the great responsibility of good works mentioned in verse 10.

"We are God's handiwork" (2:10 NEB). The Greek allows us to translate that line: "We are God's works of art." Perhaps this idea will help us grasp what it means to be made alive, raised, and made to sit with Christ. Those marvelous expressions of God's power and grace are all part of God's transforming us into works of art. We know what it is to work hard on a project, to try, to fail, and to try again, to pour ourselves into our work—not because we have to, but because we want to. In our labor, our skill, our time, and our love, we give life to words and wood and flour and paint and fabric and sheet metal. As Jesus said in his parables, if this is true for you, how much more is it true about God! If my neighbor can take an old, dead stick of wood and whittle it into a dog that can almost bark, how much more is God able to take dead lives, grace them with Christ, and create absolutely new life?

Now, you may ask, why haven't we talked about the most familiar lines in this passage, verses 8 and 9? Because they are a kind of interruption in the hymn Paul is singing. And because, when we read these words, we hear them more easily as comfortable old friends rather than as a joyous interruption of our death "through trespasses and sins."

Paul wants us to know that salvation is an undeserved rescue from the death he portrays in verses 1-3. There is no explanation—only God's amazing grace. We cannot even claim faith as our own. It is a gift from God, who is absolutely faithful. Nor are good works our own. They, too, are a gift from God as a way of life for those saved from death.

Discussion and Action

1. What external influences (Paul's "powers of the air") affect the way you live your life? What internal desires (Paul's "passions of the flesh") influence your life? Discuss ways you can gain control over these influences.
2. When have you experienced the kind of death Paul talks about in this passage?
3. When have you experienced the kind of new life Paul talks about? Share your experiences of God's grace in your lives. If you accomplish nothing more in this session than listening to stories of God's grace, you will have experienced Ephesians 2:1-10.
4. In what one specific way will being saved by grace through faith make a difference in your life this week? What will it mean for your family, neighbors, church? What will it mean for the global community? Share answers in the group and be ready to report back next week.
5. Admire each other's "works of art," giving thanks for the gifts God gives. Conclude by singing "Amazing Grace."

3

Unity in Christ
Ephesians 2:11-22

In Christ all barriers between people are destroyed. In Christ we are given peace and reconciliation—no matter how impossible that seems from a human point of view.

Personal Preparation

1. Read Ephesians 2:11-22. Rewrite the passage in your own words.
2. Consider your enemies: people or groups you dislike or distrust or who feel that way about you. What does the text have to say about such relationships? How are you called to live as a follower of the One who breaks down walls?

Understanding

In Paul's time, barriers existed between Jews and Gentiles. Because Gentiles did not follow Jewish dietary laws and ritual practices, including the ritual of circumcision for males, they were often excluded from fellowship with Jews. They were alienated from God's people. In his translation of Ephesians in *The Cotton Patch Version of Paul's Epistles*, Clarence Jordan modernizes 2:11-12, saying, "So then always remember that previously you Negroes, who sometimes are even called 'niggers' by thoughtless white church members, were at one time outside the Christian fellowship" (107). Paul is saying that the world in his time is divided into "we" and "they," "insiders" and "outsiders."

We all know about walls. There are necessary walls that give shelter. But the words in 2:13-18 describe a wall built to exclude certain people. This wall signifies hostility as much as the Berlin Wall did. It can represent racial barriers or immigration regulations or the railroad tracks through town.

Paul introduces a powerful image when he says that Christ has broken down the dividing wall between Gentiles and Jews. In Paul's eyes, this wall of hostility is a thing of the past. There may still be a few bricks lying around on the ground, but the wall is down. This is the action, not of a "gentle Jesus meek and mild," but of a rock-smashing Lord of Creation, who claims all of humanity as God's own.

Ephesians defines peace in terms of a Person, not a program. In the great love shown on the cross, Christ accomplished what diplomats and preachers and social scientists have been struggling to imitate—the death of hostility and the birth of reconciled relationships among people and with God. Notice that Paul does not outline a plan whereby the saints can join in breaking down walls. He simply sings about a fact already accomplished by the Messiah once and for all.

Are we so skeptical of the possibilities for peace in the world because we think first of programs for political change and second of the Person who gives peace? I wonder what would happen to my own peacemaking if I paid more attention to the Peacemaker. How much more effective would our efforts at reconciliation be if they always started at the foot of the cross?

Paul also describes Christ's work as the creation of "one new humanity" (2:15). Through Christ's death the Gentiles were included in the people of God. This does not mean that Gentiles were converted to Judaism or that Jews became like Gentiles. Rather, God created a new reality out of the two groups. Members of this "new humanity" will retain their individual characteristics. But God, through the work and rule of Christ, enables them to offer their gifts to one another and to God. What looked like the end—death on the cross—was really the beginning of this new creation. That is Paul's testimony.

Only after Paul makes sure we hear him out on peace between people does he talk about peace with God (2:16). According to Ephesians we can only be reconciled to God when, in Christ, we overcome our human divisions. Part of God's great plan for the universe is that all people be reconciled "to God in one body through the cross." This reconciliation is more than the repair of a damaged relationship. It is an altogether new relationship, which abandons bitter hostility for warm friendship.

The One who reconciles is also the One who provides access to God. The image of 2:17-18 is that of two enemies—one from far away and one from nearby—entering God's presence in worship together. Let your imagination wander through history, thinking of enemies and what it would be like for them to worship together.

Verse 19 sums up all that has gone before. Those who were once outsiders are now inside God's household. Now everyone belongs within the protective walls of God's house.

Paul makes a shift in verses 20-22. He moves from describing the church as a reconciled family in God's house to picturing the church as the house itself, the holy temple, "a dwelling place for God." But this house is far from a structure of solid bricks and mortar. It is a living organism, growing as a tree grows, increasing in every way—in size, number, maturity, glory, power. It is the kind of structure into which new members can always be built. And the newcomers are not just added on. They are built right into the structure. They become an integral part. They change and enrich the house as it once stood.

The center of this house is Christ. Some translators understand the Greek word in verse 20 to mean "cornerstone," that is, the stone on which the building rests. Other translators understand this word to mean the "keystone" or "capstone," which is the last stone to be put in place, bringing the building to completion. One pictures Christ as the foundation of the church. The other pictures Christ as the completion. Whatever the precise meaning of the term, the general intention is clear: Christ is the most important element in the church.

The church is a "demonstration plot" for how God's peace works. It is a place where the Spirit of God can be found. If only we could all recognize our congregations in those pictures all the time. I have been part of church meetings that have done everything *but* show God's peace and provide hospitality for God's Spirit. But there are also stories that give me hope.

A young seminary graduate became a pastor. A wise deacon told her early on, "We've had some problems in this church, but I'm not going to tell you all about them. You'll find out soon enough." Hoping that sometimes ignorance really is bliss, the pastor went about her job. Months later she began to hear whisperings, "I can't believe those two people are actually working together!" In her ignorance, the pastor had asked long-standing enemies to cooperate on a project. And they did. She hadn't known they were supposed to hate each other. She had just assumed they were members of the body of Christ. No, all the hurts were not healed. There was still much reconciliation to be accomplished. But, by concentrating on the work of the church instead of past problems, the church was strengthened and God was glorified.

The church is the sign of God's great mercy and God's wonderful peace. The church consists of people who were dead in sin and hostile to God and one another. God in Christ Jesus is the one to be praised for taking such poor building materials and creating a holy temple.

Discussion and Action

1. Hear reports of group members' experiences with last week's question 4. Encourage one another in the weeks ahead.

2. List contemporary "walls" that divide people. Are there racial, economic, sexual, other barriers within the church? within the community? within the country? What can your study group do to break down some of the walls in your congregation?

3. Recall the destruction of the Iron Curtain in 1989. What forces brought it down? What role did the Holy Spirit play in the reconciliation of Eastern and Western Europe?

4. In light of Ephesians 2:11-22, outline a letter to the editor of your local newspaper, in which you address a situation of hostility in your community, in the nation, or in the world. Assign someone to finish the letter and send it.

5. Share your own stories of how you have experienced reconciliation with others. Reflect on how that reconciliation affected your relationship with God.

6. Consider Ephesians 2:22 as an evangelism text. How well does your congregation include new members?

4

Stewards of the Mystery
Ephesians 3:1-13

Testifying to the mystery of Christ and God's plan for peace and unity, the church is a witness to the forces of this world that try to divide and conquer.

Personal Preparation

1. Read Ephesians 3:1-13, looking for clues to the "mystery" Paul writes about.
2. Do you enjoy reading mysteries or solving puzzles? Do you enjoy keeping secrets, or do you just have to tell somebody? What are the great mysteries of our time? Will they ever be solved?
3. In these verses Paul outlines his job description as a Christian. Write out your own job description. What tasks has God given you to do?

Understanding

Ephesians 3 begins and ends as a prayer of intercession for the readers. The prayer is interrupted, however, by a long parenthesis, stretching from verse 2 to verse 13. In this "aside," Paul repeats and summarizes all that he has written before. This time, though, he talks about God's plan for all creation as a revealed mystery (vv. 3, 4, 9; see also Eph. 1:9).

We usually think of a mystery as a puzzle to be solved. When we read mystery novels we read wide awake, alert and eager to pick up clues the author might have given, hoping to solve the mystery before the last page of the book. For some, this is great entertainment. Others prefer the world to be more straightforward and obvious.

Or, when we simply cannot explain something, we throw up our hands and say, "It's a mystery to me." Young children will keep asking why. With maturity sometimes comes an ability to allow some things to remain unexplained. We can even appreciate mystery in terms of not feeling compelled to understand everything— not having to figure it all out.

The mystery Paul talks about is neither a puzzle nor a series of unanswerable questions. It is something hidden, to be revealed in God's own time. A better translation for mystery is "secret." And the secret has now been made known to Paul. Indeed, it is to be made known by the church throughout the world.

New Testament scholar Markus Barth says of the term *mystery* in Ephesians 1:9:

> This is the secret that is finally revealed to the saints: God loved them before the creation. He loves them despite their sins and death. He loves them notwithstanding the former division of Jews and Gentiles. He loves them with the intention that they praise his glory. Man did not know this love; the powers did not. But God did. It was God's secret because it was hidden in his heart, identified with his own being, his whole self. Now it has been laid bare. The whole, true God is no longer hidden and unknown. His very heart is opened. (*Ephesians 1—3*, 127)

The core of God's secret is Christ and how in Christ all people are incorporated into God's people.

In 3:6 Paul claims that the "mystery of Christ" is uncovered when we come into a relationship with Jesus. In the Greek, the terms describing Gentiles all begin with the word *with*. Paul calls the Gentiles "with-heirs, with-body, and with-partakers." Gentiles are "with" God's people in the same way the saints are "with Christ" in Ephesians 2:5-6, where a similar series of three "with-" words describes how believers are made alive, raised, and seated together with Christ. Now the people who had no hope, who were without God, who seemed to belong nowhere in God's plan, find themselves joined with the body, which is none other than Christ's body.

In 3:9-10 Paul again makes clear that the mystery of God is not a secret to be kept hidden, but a glorious plan to be shared. That is the job of the church. Today we call it evangelism. The aim of evangelism in Ephesians is not to call people into a solitary faith, not even to bring them into a "personal relationship with Jesus." Rather, evangelism means calling people into God's new community and inviting them to be a part of God's work in the world. The very existence of the church as a community made up of former enemies was already in Paul's time a visible sign that God had created something radically new. The church was living proof that reconciliation and unity were possible in the midst of a broken world.

Small and powerless in the eyes of the world, Paul still saw that the church had been given the job of witnessing to the "principalities and powers." We have seen that the worldview of the first century placed these powers in the atmosphere above the earth somewhere. In today's world we understand the principalities and powers to be the institutions and structures of society, as well as any other forces (political, social, cultural, religious) that exercise dominion over people. The church is to be an example to all creation. The church is to be a servant to the world, giving all a chance to see God's plan lived out "in the flesh." The church's job is to let God's light shine in the darkness.

When the text says in verse 3:10 that God's plan "might now be made known," we might first assume that to make God "known" would be simply to announce the fact of God's existence. If that is the case, the church's job is about done. According to Gallup polls, almost everyone in our part of the world believes in the existence of God. It must take more than that to make a difference in the world.

According to the biblical tradition, knowledge involves much more than "knowing something in my head." To know God is a way of life. According to Isaiah 11:1-9, when the people practice righteousness and justice, "the earth will be full of the knowledge of the LORD as the waters cover the sea." The task of the church is to live out God's plan in such a way that it might change the principalities and powers. The church's job is to be God's agent for bringing salvation not just to individual souls but to the entire creation.

In and around Paul's discussion of God's mystery and its demonstration by the church are many references to Paul's ministry. He calls himself a prisoner for Christ. He talks about being given the stewardship of God's grace. He is not afraid of mentioning his own insight but, at the same time, calls himself the "very least" of all the saints. He identifies his ministry as being able to preach to the Gentiles about being included in God's love and God's people.

Once again he uses the word *grace* to describe God's activity. This time grace does not so much mean God's personal favor as it means having been given the gift of a ministry, a job to do. Grace is not a warm feeling we may just soak in as sunshine. Rather, it is the gift of an assignment. It is something entrusted to one person for distribution to and use by many others.

Once again grace and power are linked (as in 2:1-10). The power of God took hold of a former enemy of Christ and the church (Paul). God's grace gave him the job of working among others who were hostile to God and to one another. Paul's performance of that ministry then landed him in prison.

This long aside concludes on a note of triumph, even amid suffering and with a monumental task ahead. Paul reminds his readers of the eternal purpose of God and of the access they have to God through Christ. The boldness and confidence of believers (3:12) comes not because of their own faith but because of the faithfulness of Christ, who gives us access to the One who has set in motion this marvelous plan for the universe—and who gives each believer a part to play.

Discussion and Action

1. Take a few minutes for group members to share their experiences with mysteries, puzzles, and keeping secrets. How do those experiences inform you as you consider the "mystery of Christ"?
2. Share the job descriptions you wrote as you prepared for this class session. Affirm and support one another in the listing of abilities and tasks.
3. What does it mean in your group or congregation to be "with" one another as in verse 6? Give specific examples. On a scale of 1 to 10, rate your congregation's effectiveness in being an example of Christ's unity to all creation. Are there ways to improve your rating?
4. Reflect on the lesson's definition of evangelism: "calling people into God's new community and inviting them to be

a part of God's work in the world." What is your definition of evangelism?

5. Do you know anyone in prison for the sake of Christ and the church? Under what circumstances would you risk prison for the sake of your convictions? Amnesty International can help you speak on behalf of prisoners of conscience.

5

Rooted and Grounded in Love
Ephesians 3:14-21

This text is a prayer on our behalf—that we may receive inner resources sufficient for ministry and that we may know the love of Christ.

Personal Preparation

1. Read Ephesians 3:14-21 as Paul's prayer for you. Then use it as a guide for prayer for someone else.
2. Recall your experience with intercessory prayer—as one who has prayed on behalf of others or as one for whom the community has prayed.
3. List the images of God that you find in this prayer. How do they compare with your own images of God when you pray? How do you address God when you pray?

Understanding

Paul has been praying for the readers of Ephesians since the beginning of the letter (1:15ff.). Intercession is one of the few ministries the Apostle can still carry out while in prison. Not only does Paul pray for the churches of Asia Minor, he also lets them know of that fact by including his prayers in this letter. And so, as he concludes the devotional portion of Ephesians, Paul draws his prayer to a close as well.

This is a special prayer. It is marked by literal or figurative "bowing the knees" before God. Nearly all New Testament refer-

ences to the posture of prayer suggest that most people stood to pray.
Gentile readers would understand that one approached high authori-
ties (as well as creditors, masters, and gods) on one's knees. It is a
posture of utter humiliation which Paul adopts on behalf of his readers.

The prayer of Ephesians 1 is a prayer for spiritual enlightenment
and understanding for the whole community. The prayer of Ephesians 3 asks for spiritual power and strength for each believer. In
the first two chapters we have seen references to God's power to
give life, break down walls, and reconcile all people. Now we have
a picture of God's power working from the inside out—strengthening the believer's interior life as well as changing the exterior world
of relationships.

What is this "inner being" (3:16)? Greeks would have understood
the inner self as having to do with reason, logic, and the higher
aspects of one's personality. We will better understand the inner
self of the biblical tradition if we look at the petitions of verses
3:16-17: " . . . be strengthened in your inner being" and " . . . that
Christ may dwell in your hearts." I doubt that Paul is writing about
two different compartments in one's personhood. Rather, he is
trying to say similar things twice—asking twice for God's power
to work mightily in all facets of a believer's life.

If *inner being* is not a common biblical term, *the heart* is. The
heart is a person's source of thought and reflection. The heart is the
seat of wisdom and discernment. It also represents conscience and
will. The heart is familiar with deep emotions but is more often
connected with ideas of vitality, intelligence, and decision-making.
The heart also refers to those things that are simply inaccessible,
deeply hidden from public view. The heart represents the totality of
a person and especially the interior life. (You may wish to use a
Bible concordance to help you find references to the heart.)

So, Paul prays that each reader might be invaded and invigorated
by God's power so completely that Christ could be said to be living
in each heart and directing the whole course of each life. Next, Paul
prays that each believer might receive the power to "know the love
of Christ" and to "be filled with all the fullness of God" (3:19). But
there is a prerequisite for this knowledge: "being rooted and
grounded in love" (3:17).

Anyone who farms or gardens or keeps a plant on an office desk
knows the importance of the soil in which a living thing grows.
Anyone who has tried to remove a tree or pull up dandelions or

transplant tiny seedlings knows how vital a root system is—and how stubbornly a good one can resist all human efforts. With roots firmly anchored in the soil of love, one is prepared to face anything life has to offer. Or, in Clarence Jordan's paraphrase, with "love [as] your tap root," one is poised to be nourished with deep resources and held firm for growth to come.

The reference to being grounded in love reminds us of the picture of the church as a building being constructed as God's dwelling place (2:20-22). The prayer is that love might be the solid ground on which the temple is built, or that love might be the foundation stones themselves. Only those who are so well anchored and supported are ready for the power to understand Christ's love.

Paul is ready now to pray that the readers might be blessed with knowledge and understanding and the fullness of God. But what words does one use to describe such things? He "pulls out all the stops" in 3:18. The extent of Christ's love is too great to be fully grasped. Just imagine any dimension of space—and Christ's love is there. Paul even adds "depth" to the three dimensions (breadth, length, and height) known to geometry. Perhaps today an apostle would write about looking out into deepest space with the most modern telescope and still not see beyond Christ's love, or looking inside the tiniest cell with the most advanced microscope and not find even the most minute bit of matter or energy not loved in Christ. Paul's prayer is not so much that the readers rationally comprehend that much love, but that they appreciate the vastness of the love focused in Christ, available to the world and at work in their lives. This love surpasses knowledge and is the "stuff" of what it means to be filled with all the fullness of God.

There is a sense of being "on the way" in this prayer, a sense of the church's growing and becoming. The sense of Ephesians is that God is still in the business of creation in the great work of reconciliation—and the church is part of that process. Believers have not been rooted and grounded in love just to stay unchanged in one place, but to grow upward and outward as the body of Christ, to include all of God's people.

And that brings us to the last point about Paul's prayer. Even with all of Paul's concern for the strengthening of the interior life, still God's activity can only be understood in the company of "all the saints." Covenant groups learn about that each time they meet. Even our most intimate and personal learnings about faith have their context in the fellowship of believers—from the early Christians who told and retold the stories about Jesus to the sister or brother who holds your hand as you pray together in your covenant group.

Paul concludes this section with a doxology, a song of praise to God. Once again he sings of God's power, the power that is at work within us and yet is available to do more than we can comprehend. In the next three chapters we will see more of what God wants to do at work within us. For now, it is enough to sing glory, to worship, and to praise in response to God's love and grace and power.

Discussion and Action

1. Listen as group members report their experiences with intercessory prayer, both answered and unanswered. What affirmations can you make about the value of such prayer?
2. Make a list of people for whom you will pray this week. Include those in your congregation, community, and world.
3. Share with one another your images of God and the ways in which you address God when you pray.
4. For centuries Christians have used various disciplines to nurture their spiritual lives and to open themselves to God's power and guidance. Some of these include prayer, meditation, Bible study, fasting, solitude and retreat, worship, journal keeping, working with a spiritual director, and celebration. Which of these disciplines have been used by people in your group? What have been the results? Is there a discipline your group would choose to undertake together as a way of allowing God to strengthen your inner lives and your life together?
5. As a review, reflect on your study of the first three chapters of Ephesians. What new things have you learned about the Bible, about yourself, about others in your group?
6. Close by kneeling together in prayer if you are able.

6

Christ's Gifted Program
Ephesians 4:1-16

The church is called to live in unity and, at the same time, to use its diverse gifts to grow and mature as the body of Christ.

Personal Preparation

1. As you read Ephesians 4:1-16, consider the gift of ministry God has given you. Make a list of your gifts and consider how you are using them.
2. What gifts do you recognize in members of your covenant group? How could the gifts of the group be used more fully?

Understanding

In Ephesians 4 the focus of the letter changes. Chapters 1—3 were expressions of praise for God's plan for the universe. Now the focus narrows and Paul exhorts the readers to live like people who know they have a part in God's drama. Ephesians 4:1 shows the direct connection between ethics (the conduct of community and individual) and doctrine, or theology (the praise of God). Having witnessed to the glory of God, Paul says, "I therefore" or "I then" live accordingly. We know in our own lives that being on good behavior because of rules and regulations is much harder than finding oneself being good in the process of praising and serving God and neighbor. All of Paul's instructions about human conduct in chapters 4—6 depend upon his singing about God's grace and salvation in the first three chapters.

Our lesson issues two calls to the church: a call to unity (4:1-6) and a call to growth (4:7-16). It is one thing to wax eloquent about the church's calling to show forth God's plan of unity for the whole world. It is quite another to live out that unity in a local congregation with real people who get on one another's nerves and say hurtful things and "don't appreciate me like they should." Nevertheless, Ephesians pleads for the believers to live together in unity.

Paul honors the readers by expecting them to live up to the highest standard he knows. The Christian life is a vocation, a calling, a high responsibility. As I think of saints in the church, I remember those who considered the Christian life to be a calling that they were privileged to have been given. That kind of attitude results in the qualities listed in 4:2-3. And those are the people who helped maintain the unity of the Christian fellowship.

The basis of unity in the church is love among the believers that bears testimony to the love of God in Christ. Paul begins and ends this section by calling for the believers to be "in love"—to forbear one another in love (v. 2), to speak the truth in love (v. 15), and to be built up in love (v. 16). Members of covenant groups know that love is often hard work. There is some chance that everyone in your group is always congenial and compatible. But the People of the Covenant program was designed to provide a structure that holds people together in love and commitment, even when members are not on their best behavior and especially when there are burdens to be shared.

The love Ephesians calls for is shared among the saints. It is directed toward those with whom the believer is in contact. It has to do with the nitty-gritty of everyday living in close quarters. Love that cares for those who are a problem, love that defers to those who cause trouble, is not cheap or natural. That kind of love is not an abstract virtue. It is the product of much effort and, in the final analysis, it is a miracle of God.

We all wince in recognition when the "Peanuts" cartoon says, "I love mankind [sic]—it's people I can't stand." And yet we know that loving all humanity will not do much for maintaining the unity of a local fellowship. For that, we need the qualities of lowliness, meekness, long-suffering, and bearing one another in love.

Paul issues a call to unity, reminding the believers of their oneness in Christ. It is surely not accidental that the word *one* is used seven times in 4:4-6, since the number seven symbolizes perfection and wholeness.

Building on the theme of unity, Paul calls on the church to grow (4:7-16), using the gift of grace given to each believer. Verse 7 reminds us that each believer is given grace—not in grudging amounts, but in proportion to the sacrifice of Christ. And this gift is not for the comfort and ease of the believer. It is a ministry to be carried out for the sake of the church and the world. Verse 11 lists some specific gifts of people who carry out various roles in the church.

Here I am puzzled. Why would Paul say in verse 7 that grace was given to all and then in verse 11 list only certain church leaders? Perhaps he wrote that way to show that the gift of one grace finds expression in many different forms. Perhaps he wanted to show that Christ gives people instead of impersonal services to the church. Perhaps he wanted to show that the fledgling organization of church leadership at the time was given by God. Perhaps he meant that each believer has a quality or two of an apostle, a prophet, an evangelist, or teachers and pastors. What do you think?

Despite the reference in verse 11 to individuals we tend to identify as "clergy," verse 12 affirms that Christ equips all the saints for the work of ministry. Paul says that *all* believers share the responsibility of building up the church and are therefore saints. Some individuals may be pastors, but all are ministers. This is what is meant by the term *priesthood of all believers*. The Good News Bible emphasizes this by translating verse 12 as a separate sentence: "He did this to prepare all God's people for the work of Christian service, in order to build up the body of Christ."

The NRSV speaks of "equipping the saints." To be equipped as a saint has nothing to do with the equipment one puts on or carries. The Greek verb translated "equip" has to do with restoring, creating, or preparing (as in reconciling opposing parties or setting bones in surgery). To be equipped is the action by which a person is properly conditioned or prepared for a task ahead.

The task ahead is growth. Paul calls up various images: a body growing in size and strength, a person growing in maturity, a believer growing "into Christ." Each of these images is applied to the church as a whole. Of course, growth of the church implies growth of individuals, but the emphasis here is on the body growing into the fullness of Christ.

Evidently there was some problem in the churches with false teachers (4:14). But Paul counts on the fact that when a fellowship is united in the bonds of peace and is growing toward Christ, it can withstand the threat of heresy. Once again Paul speaks of love as the measuring stick for the church. "Speaking the truth in love" will guard against false teaching. And love is the building plan for the church.

No architect would rely on something as ill-defined as love to provide the plans for a building. And yet, the structure Paul writes about is the place in which God will dwell (2:22). It is toward this purpose that the church lives and serves. It is to God's glory that its members offer their gifts.

Discussion and Action

1. When have you felt most at home in a group? In other words, where have you experienced the most unity in a group? What factors contributed to that unity?

2. Would you rather belong to a group in which most of the people were alike or do you prefer diversity? How does a group achieve unity while allowing for diversity?

3. Consider the words *unity* and *uniformity*. Can you point to times when the church has forgotten the difference between the two? To what extent does one depend upon the other?

4. What is the biggest obstacle to unity in your congregation? in your denomination? among all Christians? What can you do to address that obstacle?

    Assign someone to interview a person involved with the local ministerial association or council of churches to get his or her views on unity. Find out how the group achieved unity. Ask about the group's hopes and plans for the future.

5. Discuss the distinction between clergy and laity in your congregation. Do laypeople in your congregation consider themselves ministers? Do they participate in the ministry of the church?

6. What has it meant in your group to "speak the truth in love"? Reflect on the sometimes uneasy relationship of truth and love.

7. Close by naming the gifts for ministry of each person in your group. Each person should write down one gift that the person to her or his left has for the ministry. Reflect on the ways your covenant group can be a training ground for these gifts. You may want to close by standing together in a circle to read aloud the gifts of your group members.

7

A Whole New Way of Living
Ephesians 4:17—5:20

In this long instructional section, we highlight the importance of imitating God. All other ethical decisions are guided by this.

Personal Preparation
1. Read this long assignment several times. Jot down the major concerns of the passage.
2. Which of these instructions most clearly apply to you?
3. Reflect on the title of this lesson, "A Whole New Way of Living." Can you point to a time in your life when you began a new way of living? Did it last long? Why or why not?

Understanding
As I write, Ben is two years old. His days are fairly evenly divided between asserting his independence and doing his best to imitate those he loves. The trick in parenting these days is to be winsome enough so that a two-year-old *wants* to do those things that make for safety and health and family harmony.

Some days I wonder if I'm any more than two years old in my spiritual life. I certainly want God to run the world my way. But, if there is hope in feeling like a spiritual two-year-old, it is in the inclination to imitate. If only we imitate the right one.

Paul is writing to new Christians in young churches. He may not know them personally, but he feels a great burden of care and responsibility for them. In today's lesson we read his instructions on correct conduct. "Do this." "Don't do that." It is an overwhelming list. But all the ethical admonitions are summed up in the curious command, "Be imitators of God, as beloved children" (5:1).

This is the only biblical text that commands us to "be imitators of God." (This passage may call to mind the statement in the Sermon on the Mount that "you, therefore, must be perfect, as your heavenly Father is perfect.") We are more familiar with instructions to imitate or follow Christ (e.g., 1 Th. 1:6; 1 Pet. 2:21; Matt. 16:24). What does it mean to imitate God?

We talk about "playing God" when there are life-and-death decisions to be made about medical treatment. We "play God" whenever we take control over another person's life. But that is not the kind of imitation Paul writes about. To imitate God is to "live in love" as Christ did (5:2). We surely cannot copy God in the work of creation or redemption. But we are called to walk the path of love, marked out by Christ. And Ephesians assumes that even youngsters in the faith can follow that path.

It is a path marked by newness of life, by singing and making melody to the Lord (5:19). It is the path of correct conduct, but also of thanksgiving. It is a path for God's beloved, forgiven children, who have been set free from bondage to former ways of life and raised from death to new life with Christ.

It does sound pretentious to talk about imitating God—as if we could live up to some abstract, ideal standard of behavior, as if by our own good intentions we could be like God. But that is not the flavor of Ephesians. Believers are "beloved children"—those whom God has already chosen and loved. Their actions are to flow from the grace God has already given. For example, Paul calls us to forgive others as God in Christ already forgave us (4:32). It is not our job to "play God." It is our job to live in love and so imitate the One who first loved us.

Ephesians knows that a new day has dawned for the believers. The darkness of past alienation and sin is over. In dramatic fashion they have been given a new life. Now they must learn to live out that new life without slipping back into old habits. The image Paul uses is that of taking off and putting on clothing.

In early Christian teaching, it was a common figure of speech to talk about "putting off" evil behaviors as if they were old clothes not suited to one's new life. Perhaps this came from the practice at baptism of discarding old clothes and receiving new, white garments. Clothing can symbolize or reflect inner feelings. We tell the world about our values by the way we dress. Even as we decide what to wear today, we decide whether to cling to the old person or to allow ourselves to be renewed and put on the new nature which is God's gift.

There is no room here for the excuses we make for our shortcomings. Ephesians assumes that change is possible—not by human power, but by God's power. Clothed in God's righteousness and holiness, we are urged to put away our former ways of life.

Ephesians 4:25 recalls the earlier words about speaking the truth in love. The setting for such speech is the Christian community. In the church it is often tempting to be nice and put up with one another. But Paul instructs us to speak the truth and to deal with anger. That is the way to the reconciliation promised in Ephesians 2. In being honest and forthright with one another, believers are invited to participate in authentic unity that goes beyond polite concern for one another. Paul knows that life in any community is painful as well as joyful. But when that community is rooted and grounded in the love of Christ, its participants are empowered to work through their anger and hurt as members of one another. The grand and glorious vision of church unity cannot be maintained by silence or falsehood.

These verses in the Revised Standard Version (RSV) make a great deal of "walking" and "talking." When Paul gives instructions for "walking," they are instructions for one's whole way of living. The walk Paul envisions is no meaningless meandering. It is a journey on a path God has marked. It evokes memories of the Hebrews walking out of Egypt, led by a pillar of cloud and fire. It reminds us of Jesus' instructions to follow him, cross and all. The believers are to walk in love, to walk as children of light, and to walk as wise people.

Then there is the matter of "talking." Notice how many instructions in these verses have to do with what the believers say. Even to mention evil things by name is as much as to make them present and take responsibility for them (5:3). We cannot overestimate the importance of the speech we share with one another. I'm reminded of a story about a visiting preacher who was invited to speak at a certain church on Temperance Sunday. But instead of talking about the evils of alcohol, he preached a powerful sermon on the evil of gossip. He said that was the message the Christians really needed to hear.

In Ephesians, gratitude is the basis of ethics. Love might tell us how we ought to act, but gratitude provides the motivation. Thanksgiving crowds out silly, destructive talk. And, of course, true thanksgiving does not come in a long, sober face. It comes singing.

Discussion and Action

1. Share your initial reactions to the lists of do's and don'ts in Ephesians 4:17—5:20.
2. Decide which sections of the assigned scripture are most important for your group to discuss. Spend several minutes working on those sections, asking questions of one another and seeking implications of Paul's instructions for your life today.
3. Then take a break. Play the children's game of "Follow the Leader" for a few minutes. Pay attention to how you feel about imitating someone else—and how you feel about leading. Share those reactions with the group. How do they compare with your initial reactions to this lesson?
4. Consider the instruction to imitate God. What is your group's reaction to that instruction?
5. Listen as each person shares a practical implication of the Christian walk—a change he has had to make in the past, one she is working on in the present, or one she needs to make in the future. How can you help each other "walk carefully" in the days ahead?
6. Conclude by writing a litany of thanksgiving. Include in your litany things for which you are thankful in your family, your covenant group, and your congregation.

8

Submission in Christ
Ephesians 5:21-33

Ephesians gives us a new pattern for relating as wives and husbands: mutual subordination. "Reverence for Christ," and not the status quo, is the guideline for Christian relationships.

Personal Preparation
1. Read Ephesians 5:21-33 and write a paraphrase.
2. Consult a Bible dictionary for information about the roles of women and men in the first century.
3. If your church library or someone in your congregation has a copy, read chapter 8, "The Discipline of Submission," in Richard J. Foster's *Celebration of Discipline* (Harper & Row, 1988).

Understanding
When I was growing up, one of the rules of the house was a schedule for washing dishes. My days were Wednesdays and Saturdays. I will go to my grave with a slight dread of Wednesday evenings because those were dishwashing nights—even though my turn comes much more often now as one of only two dish washers in the family.

We all remember "rules of the house" from our growing-up years. Some were posted on the refrigerator or kitchen door. Some were just understood: "This is the way we do things in our house." One of the biggest challenges in establishing homes of our own—as single people, couples, or parents of children—is to decide what rules apply in this new house.

Today's lesson focuses on what scholars call a "household code." These household codes, which listed rules for how to act in the family, were a common instructional tool in the Greek world. They were adopted and modified by the early church to instruct converts (see Col. 3:18—4:1; 1 Pet. 2:13—3:7; Tit. 2:1-10; 1 Tim. 2:8-15; 6:1-2). This week we will study Paul's instructions for married couples. Next week we will look at rules for children and parents, slaves and masters. Now we put to the test the theology and doctrine Paul has been writing about: Do Christ and the community of faith have anything to do with the most intimate and critical areas of personal, daily life?

This household code begins with a surprising call to mutual subordination. In the first century, men had power and legal standing. For the most part, women had only secondary status. But Paul addresses the husbands and wives, who are members of Christ's body, as equal partners in the gospel, called to "give way to one another" (JB) out of reverence for Christ.

This passage is a "red flag" text for many. It raises problems for many of us because we simply don't want anyone telling us to subordinate ourselves. Period. We don't want to give way to another person or government or custom or scripture. Additionally, 5:22 has often been pulled out of context either to "keep women in their place" or to prove what a chauvinist Paul was. Today's challenge is to study Ephesians 5:21-33 with as little prejudice as possible in order to hear the message for the first readers and for us.

The thesis is this: "Be subject to one another out of reverence for Christ" (5:21). Everything that follows serves to illustrate the premise that the basic relationship of all Christians is humble subordination to one another. The basis of this passage is neither control nor power, but love. To describe a voluntary attitude of cooperation, Paul uses the Greek word *hypotasso* ("subordinate" is a better translation of this word than "be subject") with regard to Christ and all the saints, wives, children, and slaves. It is something he expects only of Christ and of those in Christ. The women and men of Christ's body are called on to serve one another voluntarily out of reverence for Christ who came "not to be served but to serve" (Matt. 20:28). The phrase "out of reverence for Christ" reminds us that the problems of interpersonal relationships, whether in this household code or not, cannot be solved by human reason and human standards alone.

Ephesians 5:22-24 is addressed to the wives in the churches and not to women in general. Now, why would people who are already without power and status be told to subordinate themselves? In light of the gospel that Paul had been preaching in Ephesians, those old walls of custom and sin had been broken down in Christ. Now the sisters as well as Gentiles were full members of Christ's body. And so they could be addressed as free moral agents, as dignified and respected members of the people chosen by God.

A wife is to subordinate herself to her husband as "head." We assume we know very well what head means. We assume that the head makes the decisions for the body. The head is the boss. But, in biblical times, people thought decisions were made in the heart. The head had to do with "origin" or "source," as in the "head of a river." According to Ephesians 4:15-16, Christ as head of the church causes the church to grow, knits the church into a unity, nourishes each member, and gives strength so that the church might build itself up in love. It is a headship of love, not of control. With regard to wives and husbands, Paul was probably thinking back to Gen. 2:18-23 where the woman had her origins in man, as the church has its origins in Christ.

Ephesians 5:25-33 is addressed to the marriage partner with the legal power and status. The first thing the husband is told to do is to love his wife the way Christ loved the church—to give himself up for her. Three times Paul tells husbands to love their wives. This is the revolutionary part of the text. Men did not marry for love. They married for convenience, for economic reasons, for procreation. No wonder Paul had to take twice as much space to instruct husbands as wives. It was the husbands who were called on to make the big changes. They were to love their wives with agape-love, God-love, self-sacrificing love.

Ephesians 5 is a joyful affirmation of all aspects of marriage as part of God's new creation. It is not a relationship bound by the social expectations of the time. But it is marked by order—subordination of one's own wishes to the other partner. Both wives and husbands are given the privilege of imitating Christ in the context of their marriage—serving and loving one another. The words of instruction may be different for each spouse, but the motivation and example are the same: the life and love of Christ.

What place does such a household code have in our own lives? We all recognize the need for patterns in every culture, every relationship, every organism. Much of the beauty of life comes from patterns we can count on—whether in quilt blocks or on computer paper or in a marriage relationship. We look for patterns that are useful and workable and life-enhancing.

Traditionally, the pattern in marriage was that the wife gave the most in terms of her own personhood in order to make a family "work." She gave up her name, her autonomy, her creativity for the good of husband and children. The church encouraged this, reading only the first few words of Ephesians 5:22, among other New Testament texts. That pattern was workable and useful to society, but it was often not life-enhancing for the sister.

In the past decades, that pattern has been severely disrupted. There is deep fear among some that without traditional patterns the world as we know it will fall apart. And we are daily witnesses to many changes that have come in families and society because old patterns have disappeared. We look anxiously into the future for a new pattern that will give family and society stability and nurture and be life-enhancing to all its members. Ephesians 5 gives us a place to start searching for such a pattern, a pattern of service and love.

Discussion and Action

1. Listen as each person shares two "rules of the house" from childhood. What rules have they adopted in their own homes?
2. Listen as each person shares an image of a model marriage. Where have you seen such a relationship? What contributed to the success of that marriage?
3. Discuss the meaning of the term *subordination*. Is this a workable model for modern marriages? Why or why not?
4. Roleplay a husband and wife at breakfast making plans for the day: first, with the husband "in charge," then with the wife "in charge," and finally with each seeking to serve the other. How are decisions made? How are duties divided?
5. Consider ways your congregation can act to nurture marital relationships.
6. Consider ways you can assist people caught in destructive and abusive marriages. A shelter for battered spouses and children can always use donations and volunteers. Are

there ways the church has either failed to nurture marriages or contributed in negative ways to the ill health of marriage relationships?

7. Consider making a gift for a couple about to be married or celebrating an anniversary.

9

Who's In Charge Here?
Ephesians 6:1-9

With regard to relationships of "superiors" and "inferiors," Paul offers a new look at issues of authority and obedience.

Personal Preparation

1. As you read Ephesians 6:1-9, consider your experience as a child. How did your parents exasperate you? What do you most appreciate about the way you were brought up?
2. Consider your work experience. Who was your best boss? Why?

Understanding

Anyone who has ever worked with children has had this experience. You tell child to do something. "Why?" You give a reasonable explanation. The child does not move. You give several reasonable explanations. Finally you thunder: "You'll do it because I said so!" The look in your eye, the set of your jaw, the tone of your voice make it clear that that is reason enough. We are not often proud of ourselves when we resort to that tactic. But in the moment we do not know another way to go. We use raw power and authority over someone younger and smaller.

Questions of authority and obedience are at the heart of today's lesson. Those "in Christ" are to handle authority and give obedience in a way quite different from those in the world around them.

Paul wrote Ephesians 6:1-9 against a social background in which fathers, as heads of households, had absolute power over the members of their households, including both children and slaves. Most first-century teachers of ethics gave instruction to free men, telling them how to make society run smoothly. But Paul addresses both children and slaves as responsible members of the faith community.

First he speaks to children. I wish I knew how old these "children" were. Every culture has its own definition of when childhood ends and the responsibilities of adulthood begin. By any standard, however, children are those who are vulnerable in terms of size, ability, experience, and power. Children are expected to obey "just because." But Paul gives four reasons for obedience—it is right, it is commanded, it leads to happiness and long life. At least one of these should appeal to the "child" of any age.

Some interpreters believe that obedience "in the Lord" means obeying only in cases covered by scripture. It is as if they are looking for a loophole as quickly as possible or following the rules precisely in order to qualify as a Christian. But it seems to be more consistent with the message of Ephesians to obey "*because* you are a Christian" or "as a Christian should." Paul is talking about a new spirit of obedience as part of a transformed relationship "in Christ."

Paul asks that children freely obey their parents to honor God's plan of salvation for the whole universe. And he instructs fathers to guide and nurture their children with gentleness and restraint. As the NIV translates it, fathers are not to "exasperate" their children. Even though a father had the legal right to do whatever he pleased with his children, Ephesians counsels respect and care for them. Indeed, he is to "bring them up" in the same way that Christ nurtures the church.

In today's world we might apply this message to both fathers and mothers, though it was directed only to fathers in the letter. This is another case in which the Christian way of relating radically restricts the power a superior person may use over an inferior. The male parent, like the male spouse, was the one with the power in Ephesus, and Ephesians makes it quite clear that that power is to be used on behalf of the one who is more vulnerable.

Mothers and fathers are to use their authority as parents to bring up their children "in the nurture and admonition of the Lord" (KJV). I remember that beautiful phrase from the service of baby dedication. It is the foundation of education in the Christian home. Modern translations talk about discipline (training) and instruction, once again, in the context of life in the Lord. As the rules for behavior in the home are passed on from one generation to another, so are the understandings and responsibilities of faith.

Any discussion of parent-child relationships brings back many memories and "gets our emotional juices flowing." We are all experts in terms of our own experience in this area. We do not have the same kind of experience, however, when it comes to the relationship of master and slave.

In the first century, slavery was an integral part of society. People became slaves after their homeland was conquered by the Roman army or when they could not pay their debts. Although the law regarded a slave as a "tool that could talk," many slaves were well educated and performed important roles in society, for example, as teachers or physicians. Again, the question is what it means to be a Christian in a relationship where one person has all the power and the other person has none. Paul puts the master/slave relationship in a new perspective. Slaves are slaves of Christ and are instructed to conduct their daily lives in that light. Masters have a master in heaven who treats everyone the same. The supposedly high and the supposedly low are all subject to the same highest authority.

In every verse of the instructions to slaves, Christ or "the Lord" is mentioned. In this context Paul calls for a new kind of obedience, one that springs from service and not servitude. He identifies work as a ministry whose model and object is Christ. Suddenly obedience is not something one is compelled to give, but it is one's ministry. The Christian slave is given the privilege of imitating Christ in service to the master. Obedience becomes service to Christ. Those words echo the parable of the Sheep and the Goats in Matthew 25—only this time the service is to be given not only to the "least of these" but also to the one who has the legal right to compel obedience. In the same way that Paul could find dignity and glory in imprisonment, he sees dignity and freedom in service. A slave's experience of Christ could give a whole new motivation for work and revolutionize her life within even the most difficult circumstances.

By now the instructions to the masters do not surprise us. Masters are to treat slaves as people of dignity and worth. In particular, they are not to threaten their slaves—not even in a situation where punishment could legally be swift and arbitrary. Masters are reminded that there is no distinction between people in God's sight.

And so we have come full circle, back to the beginning of this section of household rules: "Submit yourselves to one another out of reverence for Christ."

Can you see in your mind's eye a picture of the church at Ephesus listening to Paul's words? Can you see all the different people gathered: women and men, old and young, wealthy and poor, slave and master, Gentile and Jew, children and parents? Can you see their faces as it begins to sink in that this wonderful new faith is going to challenge their most basic assumptions about the relationships of daily life? Surely you will see wonder and puzzlement. You might see a flicker of fear as someone wonders "what this world is coming to." You will see a stooped back straighten with a new consciousness of dignity and worth.

Can you see in your mind's eye the faces of those with whom you interact daily (your parents, children, employer, employees, spouse, co-workers) as you try to discern the implications of Paul's words for your own life and relationships?

Discussion and Action

1. How would you respond to 6:1 as a young child? a teenager? a young adult? a middle-aged person caring for an elderly parent?
2. As a parent or one who cares for children, what is the difference between exasperating a child and setting and maintaining appropriate limits?
3. Listen as group members describe their "best boss." What is a profile of such a person? What is a profile of a "best employee"? What place does use of authority play in such profiles?
4. Where have you seen authority abused—in families, the church, society? What are the roots of such abuse? How can you be an agent of justice and healing in such situations?
5. If you are the descendant of slaves or a person oppressed because of race, class, or sex, how do you respond to Paul's instruction to be slaves of Christ? If you belong to a majority group that has always had access to power, how do you respond to Paul's teaching?
6. Do you agree that conflict is inevitable where two or more people live or work together? The church is attempting to teach people to deal with conflict in the home, congre-

gation, workplace, and larger community. If you would like to learn about training opportunities in mediation and conflict resolution, contact the Ministry of Reconciliation, On Earth Peace Assembly, P.O. Box 188, New Windsor, MD 21776.

10

The Whole Armor of God
Ephesians 6:10-24

Daily living takes strength and courage. God provides the equipment for meeting the challenges.

Personal Preparation

1. Read Ephesians 6:10-24 and consider how the "battle" is going in your life. What piece of equipment do you need most for your challenges this week?
2. List the "evils" that influence your life.
3. Find a picture of a Roman soldier or a medieval "knight in shining armor." Use it to help you visualize the text. Take it along to your covenant group meeting.

Understanding

Perhaps during the course of this study you have found yourself thinking that Ephesians is all very nice, that it holds out a wonderful vision for the church and for family relationships, but that it is just a little too ideal for the life you live. Ephesians 6:10-20 is about life in the real world—a world where marriages crumble, where children are abused and neglected, where "nice guys finish last," and where evil is a part of life.

Many of us do not think much about evil. We were taught to look for the good in people and events. We are aware of everyday temptations (chocolate chip cookies, another helping of mashed potatoes), or we have some image of a pitchfork-wielding devil that opposes things godly. But, for Paul, evil dare not be ignored or trivialized. For him, evil is real. It is personal. It has a life of its own. It affects individuals, and it works through the structures of human society. Evil is not only the result of human sinfulness. It is a separate and pervasive power in the order of life. And, oh, how the human race is inclined toward it!

The good news is that evil does not have the last word. It is not irresistible. Paul closes Ephesians by urging believers to make use of the resources God gives to resist evil, to stand firm against even the real world, knowing that God's chosen people have a different inheritance.

Paul urges the believers to be strong in the Lord. This strength is not the result of self-discipline and self-improvement. It is a gift of God. Paul uses the same words here as he did back in 1:19 to describe the power that raised Christ from the dead. Once again, resurrection power is available to all the saints.

Three sections follow. Ephesians 6:11-13 urges the believer to put on God's armor in preparation for spiritual warfare. This military image jolts us at the end of a book concerned mostly with the "gospel of peace." But the call to arms is for the purpose of standing fast—not to conquer new territory, but to hold one's position, to refuse to give ground to the forces of wickedness. It calls to mind Exodus 14:13 and the many other Old Testament references to the Lord going into battle for Israel, once Israel was prepared and obedient.

Ephesians 6:14-17 expands the metaphor of the armor God provides. Throughout the Roman Empire people would recognize this description of a Roman soldier's gear. Because this is a metaphor, we will not push the details too far. It is better to see before us a picture of a person equipped with everything necessary for the job at hand, wearing the "whole armor" (the "whole kit and caboodle"). It is God's armor. Indeed, Isaiah 59:17 gives us a picture of God dressed for battle on behalf of the people.

Since we have few Roman soldiers in our neighborhoods, it might be helpful to think of other images of a person prepared. What about a football player with pads and tape and helmet in place? What about a child bundled up to play outside in the snow? What about a business person headed for the airport with briefcase and carry-on luggage?

The tools of the believer's defense against evil are truth, righteousness, peace, faith, salvation, and the word of God. These are ways that God's power and might are available to the believer. All the saints together are to receive these as a gift of God. They face the battles ahead as people honored by grace and with full confidence in God's victory.

Ephesians 6:18-20 reminds believers that strength comes from prayer—strength for their own battles and for Paul in his. He urges them to keep alert and never give up, no matter how bleak the present situation. Paul notes his own circumstances: he is an "ambassador in chains," imprisoned by the "principalities and powers," but standing firm in the face of their onslaught. He continues to need the support of the saints in prayer, to stand, "having done everything" (6:13).

I hear what the text says about putting on God's armor to be prepared for the attack of evil. I've read enough about first-century warfare to see in my mind's eye a disciplined band of Roman soldiers protected by huge shields, unable to be driven from any spot they chose to occupy. Ephesians aims to comfort us with that image.

But most of my encounters with evil seem to be other than frontal attacks. They are more like guerilla warfare—a sniper here, a land mine there, a long night in the terrifying darkness of the soul. Armor does little good under those conditions. Or I long for a big evil to resist, some grand and glorious cause. But the nature of our world today usually means that such battles are not neat and tidy, once and done. They are usually not even exciting, often carried on in stuffy boardrooms and courtrooms and legislative chambers. The bureaucracy that makes decisions about health care for the homeless and weapons for Central America grinds away at our best intentions to stand firm in the cause of resisting evil.

And so I need to be reminded of the picture of God's holy war—God fighting the battles, God providing the equipment and the know-how. Not much in my religious past has taught me about joining in on God's side of the battle. I was taught more about peacemaking, about avoiding conflict, than about recognizing God at work there.

But Ephesians calls us to see God at work throughout the universe, throughout all of history, and in the life of each precious individual sinner-made-saint. And Ephesians calls each believer and each community of believers to join both in resisting evil and in creating God's new world. Ephesians wants to break down the walls that not only separate us from one another but define our world in manageable, bite-sized pieces. Ephesians wants us to see the world from God's point of view—both the evil and the promise.

And at the heart of it all is Christ—the humble carpenter from Nazareth, crucified on a Roman cross by the real world. Ephesians sings about what happens next: new life, resurrection, exaltation to glory—for Christ and for all the saints.

Unlike most of the Pauline letters, Ephesians does not expect the world as we know it to end soon. And so it is important for families to work out patterns for living together. It is important for the church to learn how to work as one body. And it is important for the believers never to forget that they have God's very own resources for coping with the real world. God's people are in it for the long haul. And, oh, the music God gives us to sing in the meantime!

Discussion and Action

1. As one person reads aloud Ephesians 6:10-20, the other group members may view pictures of soldiers in armor.
2. What images of preparedness would you use to deliver the message of the text today?
3. Share your lists of modern expressions of evil. What equipment do you need to oppose them?
4. How do you reconcile the images of military preparedness in the service of the One who brings peace and unity?
5. Where is God calling your covenant group to "stand firm" in your congregation, community, wider world? How will you do that job? Discuss ways in which you can maintain the energy necessary to stand firm—as a group and as individuals.
6. Review the book of Ephesians. Listen as each one summarizes the message of Ephesians for her or himself.
7. Take turns reading 6:23-24 to one another as a blessing for the end of this study. Having experienced Ephesians, listen to the music of these words with new ears.

Suggestions for Sharing and Prayer

As you meet in your small group, you will experience life in Christian community as you study the Letter to the Ephesians. You will find the scriptures speaking directly to your life together, even as they spoke to that first-century group of believers.

A sharing and prayer time can be a time for talking about how God's salvation through Jesus Christ touches your life personally. It will be a time for talking about growing in your Christian faith, for setting goals. As you share and talk, sing and pray, you will live out Christian community in your small group.

The ideas given here are to help you plan your sharing and prayer time. Choose from these ideas and add your own. May God's Spirit lead you to ever deeper moments of sharing and praying together.

1. God's Great Plan

- ❑ If your group has met together before in a previous study, you could begin your sharing and prayer time by inviting people to tell something special that has happened since your group last met. Or ask each person to name their feelings about coming together as a covenant group.

- ❑ You will probably want to spend some time checking out meeting dates and discussing your expectations for your time together.

- ❑ As you begin to think about the Ephesians study and your life as a Christian community, name one thing each of you looks forward to in meeting every week to share and pray together.

- ❑ Talk about some hymns that speak to you about God's plan of salvation through Jesus Christ. Include some Christmas hymns in your list. Then sing some of these as a group prayer. Or pray and meditate silently as you listen to recorded Christmas music.

2. Amazing Grace

❑ Share earliest memories of what the word *grace* meant to
you. Then share some stories of God's grace present in your
life most recently. Read together the "Litany of God's
Grace" (p. 56).

❑ Read the words of "Amazing Grace." Sing them as an
affirmation of faith or as a prayer. Name other hymns or
scripture verses that speak to you of God's grace.

❑ Name people and situations in today's world where God's
grace needs to be felt. Include personal, family, community,
national, and worldwide concerns. Hold these up before God
in intercessory prayer; after each concern is named, respond
with "Hear our prayer, O Lord" or "Heal your people (or
world), O God."

❑ Covenant with each other to hold these same people and
situations before God in prayer during the coming week.

3. Unity in Christ

❑ Begin sharing time by asking several of the following
questions:

a. Can you remember someone you thought was your enemy
during your school years? Why did you see this person as
enemy?

b. Name people or groups today whom it is easy to distrust
or fear. What would be needed to lessen the barriers of
fear and distrust?

c. Name a situation in which you felt like a stranger.
Describe your feelings at the time.

d. Talk about the meaning of the words of the hymn
"Strangers No More" (p. 58). Use this hymn in your
prayer time. Learn the refrain well enough to sing it
together. Then read the verses as a spoken prayer and sing
the refrain as your prayer response.

❑ For another prayer idea, have each person write on a note card a situation in which he or she feels alone or like a stranger. Seal the card in an envelope; pass all envelopes around the group, with each person taking one. Pray for this person in the specific situation during the week.

4. Stewards of the Mystery

❑ Use one or several of these ideas to begin your sharing:

a. What was your favorite mystery book as a child?

b. What is the last good mystery you read?

c. What do you like about mystery in your life? What do you dislike?

d. Name some of the mysteries that are a part of life (like those in Proverbs 30:18-19 RSV): "the way of an eagle in the sky . . . a ship on the high seas . . . a man with a maiden."

e. What mysteries are part of the life of faith?

❑ To be in personal prayer, yet praying within the community, have each person write out a "job description for me as a believer" for the coming week (or month), focusing on what God is "giving me to do in this week or month."

❑ Share your writing in pairs. Plan to pray for each other as you live out your job descriptions and check with each other regularly during the week. Or invite people to share part of their job descriptions in the total group. In a prayerful mood, speak a prayer response after each person shares: "Hear our prayer, O Lord" or other prayer response. Then sing "Lord, I Want to Be a Christian."

5. Rooted and Grounded in Love

❑ Consider these ideas for sharing about prayer, related to Paul's prayer in Ephesians 3:14-21:

a. Give the names of people and situations for whom you have prayed this past week.

b. Name hymns about prayer, or prayer hymns, that are
   important for your faith. Sing some of these. Ask each
   person to respond with a short phrase to the words
   "Prayer is . . . " After all have responded, use the hymn
   "Prayer Is the Soul's Sincere Desire" or "Guide Me, O
   Thou Great Jehovah" in one of the following ways:

   • Read the words together as an affirmation about prayer.

   • Listen prayerfully as someone sings the hymn.

   • Listen in prayer as one person reads the words. Perhaps
     have quiet music playing also.

   • Sing the hymn together.

❑ Pray together, using the words of the hymn "Breathe on Me,
   Breath of God." One person could read the words and all
   respond with "We beseech Thee, hear us." Or different
   people could read the words of each stanza, with all
   responding.

❑ Henri Nouwen talks about prayer as the movement "from
   clenched fists to open hands." Use this idea as you pray
   silently, pray aloud, or as you sing a prayer. A hymn that
   could be used is "Lord, Listen to Your Children" (p. 62). As
   you pray or sing, move from open hands to outstretched
   arms, reaching upward to God.

6. Christ's Gifted Program

❑ Focus this sharing time around a "gift bombardment." Take
   turns, with one person sitting in the center of the group, naming
   the gifts that person brings to your covenant group. One
   member of the group could list these gifts on a card as they
   are named and give it to the person. Or you could make cards
   for each person, thanking them for their gifts to the group.

❑ Consider another sharing idea: Ask people to tell about or
   describe their impressions of God or Jesus when they were
   children. Then talk about how these ideas or impressions
   have matured or deepened as they have grown older.

❑ Use clay, pipe cleaners, or building blocks to make a symbol of unity in your group or in your congregation. Share your creations and talk about their meaning.

❑ Use the hymn "Unity" as a prayer (p. 60), singing it together or using the words as your prayer for unity.

7. A Whole New Way of Living

❑ Share some of the do's and don'ts that were part of your childhood. Then name some do's and don'ts that are a part of your present home.

❑ Talk about people who were models for you when you were a child. Who are your models today? Give thanks to God for these people and their influence on your life.

❑ Look quickly through the Ephesians text you will study today; notice the many references to "talking" and "walking." Think of hymns that focus on speaking or talking about the faith; do the same for those that focus on walking with the Lord or walking in the way. Some examples:

> "Open My Eyes, That I May See" (v. 3)
> "Take My Life" (v. 3)
> "I Love To Tell the Story"
> "Lord, Speak to Me That I May Speak"
> "O Master, Let Me Walk with Thee"
> "When We Walk with the Lord"

Sing some of these hymns, choosing those that are most meaningful for you. Plan to use some of them for prayer time.

❑ Share scriptures you recall that speak about the new way of living as Christians. Give thanks for the words of Scripture that are a guide for living.

8. Submission in Christ

❑ What comes to mind as you think of submission? Why?

❑ Look at some key phrases from the hymn "Make Me a Captive, Lord." What does each say to you? Where have you experienced this truth in the past month?

> "Make me a captive, Lord,
>   and then I shall be free."

> "My heart is weak and poor
>   Till it a master find."

> "My power is faint and low
>   Till I have learned to serve."

> "My will is not my own
>   Till Thou has made it Thine."

❑ We are used to serving others. Has someone served you in some way? How? How did it feel?

❑ If your church practices feetwashing, talk about some of your feelings during feetwashing at the love feast. How does it feel to wash someone's feet? How does it feel to have your feet washed?

❑ Sing the hymn "Fill Us with Your Love" (p. 61).

❑ Kneel as you pray together, asking God for a growing understanding of submission and for the faith to live it out.

9. Who's In Charge Here?

❑ Talk about ways in which you, as children, were expected to obey your parents.

❑ Look through your hymnal for hymns that speak about children and parents and their relationship in the home. Read the words or sing some of the hymns.

❑ Sing the hymn "Come People, Celebrate and Sing" by Wilbur Brumbaugh. (Use the hymn tune from "In Christ There Is No East or West.")

Come people, celebrate and sing
    a song of liberty;
Join hand and heart in sounds of praise
    to God Who made us free.
In God the Spirit we are one,
    together bound, but free;
In God's own image we are made
    to be what each can be.

To each God gives a destiny,
    in paths that none can see;
A life unfolding fresh and free,
    to live creatively.
Praise God who freely gives to all
    abundant life at birth;
Praise God who wills that all shall live
    in dignity and worth.

❑ Name in prayer people whose God-given dignity is denied, people who are being abused by those in power. Covenant with each other to remember these people in your prayers this week.

10. The Whole Armor of God

❑ Recall the names of your heroes when you were a child or youth. Name Christian heroes who used the "whole armor of God" to battle evil in the past or to do battle with evil today.

❑ Share scriptures, other than Ephesians 6, that use battle imagery. What do these texts call you to do? Come to God in silent prayer, listening for where God would have you as a covenant group "do battle" in your community.

❑ Share scriptures that express your beliefs about God's salvation through Christ. Name hymns that also make this affirmation. Sing several of these as your closing prayer.

General Sharing and Prayer Resources

Litany of God's Grace

We gather together to ask the Lord's blessing.
But more than that.
   We are here to offer
      to confess our human frailty,
      to be challenged by God's word,
      to be open to the working of God's Spirit.
In other words,
   We call ourselves to worship—
      with the hope that as God is revealed in this hour,
   we won't be too arrogant
      or stubborn or sleepy
to hear and see what God would have us know.

By Ken Gibble, We Gather Together,
© 1979 by Brethren Press. Used by permission.

A Prayer

O God, we thank you for gifts that belong
   not to us alone,
      but to all our sisters and brothers,
         since they too are created in your image.
Let their need become our need.
   let their hunger become our hunger;
   and grant to us also a portion of their pain,
   so that in sharing ourselves we discover
      the Christ who walks with our sisters and brothers. Amen.

By Kenneth Morse, We Gather Together,
©1979 by Brethren Press. Used by permission.

An Affirmation

Lord God, we believe;
  help our unbelief.
Lord God, we believe,
  but we incline to doubt;
  help us to doubt our doubts.
Lord, we believe;
  We would be more believing;
  We would be more trusting.
  Help us to be more affirming. Amen.

Affirmation of Faith

He was the Son of God . . . He was the Son of man.
He came down from heaven . . . He was born in a stable.
Kings came to his cradle . . . His first home was a cave.
He was born to be a king . . . He was the child of Mary.
He was the greatest among men . . . He was the least among
  servants.
He was loved and honored . . . He was despised and rejected.
He was gentle and loving . . . He made many enemies.
He counseled perfection . . . He was the friend of sinners.
He was a joyful companion . . . He was a man of sorrows.

He said, "Rejoice" . . . He said, "Repent."
He said, "Love God with all your heart" . . . He said, "Love your
  neighbor as yourself."
He said, "Don't be anxious" . . . He said, "Count the cost."
He said, "Deny yourself" . . . He said, "Ask and receive."

In him was life . . . He died on the cross.
He was a historic person . . . He lives today.
He was Jesus of Nazareth . . . He is Christ the Lord.

For we are strangers no more

STRANGERS NO MORE 11 10. 11 10 with refrain

Text: Kenneth I. Morse, 1979
        Copyright ©1979 Church of the Brethren General Board
Music: Dianne Huffman Morningstar
        Copyright ©1979 Dianne Huffman Morningstar

Unity

Refrain: Je - sus, help us live in peace,
1 Man - y times we dis - a - gree
2 How we long for pow'r and fame.

from our blind - ness set us free.
o'er what's right or wrong to do.
seek - ing ev - 'ry earth - ly thing.

Fill us with your heal - ing love. _____
It's so hard to real - ly see. _____
We for - get the One who came. _____

Text: Gerald Derstine; based on Philippians 2:1-8
Music: Gerald Derstine; accomp. by Orlando Schmidt
        Text and Music copyright ©1971 by Gerald Derstine. Adapted by permission.

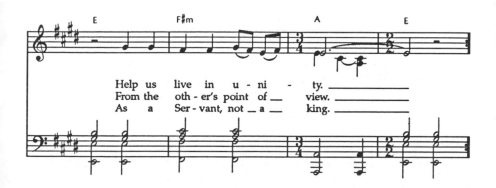

Help us live in u - ni - ty. _____
From the oth - er's point of __ view. _____
As a Ser - vant, not __ a __ king. _____

Fill us with your love

Je - su, ____ Je - su, ____ Fill us with Your love, show

us how to serve the neigh-bors we have from You. ___

1 Kneels at the feet of His friends,   Si - lent - ly wash - es their
2 Neigh-bors are rich __ and poor,   Neigh-bors are black __ and
3 These are the ones we should serve,   These are the ones we should
4 Lov - ing puts us on our knees,   Serv - ing as though we are

feet,   Mas - ter who acts as a slave __ to them.
white,   Neigh-bors are near - by and far __ a - way.
love,   All __ are neigh-bors to us __ and You.
slaves,   This is the way we should live __ with You.

Text: tr. by Tom Colvin
Music: Ghana Folk Song

Lord, listen to your children

CHILDREN PRAYING 98. 99

Lord, lis-ten to your chil-dren pray - ing,

Lord, send your Spir-it in this place.

Lord, lis-ten to your chil-dren pray - ing,

send us love, send us pow'r, send us grace!

Other Covenant Bible Studies available from *faithQuest:*

Forming Bible Study Groups
by Steve Clapp and Gerald Peterson. . . . 0-87178-293-6   C423

Abundant Living: Wellness from a Biblical Perspective
by Mary Sue Rosenberger. 0-87178-006-2   8062

Covenant People
by Shirley J. Heckman
and June A. Gibble 0-87178-169-7   8697

Disciplines for Spiritual Growth
by Karen Peterson Miller 0-87178-812-8   8128

1 Corinthians: The Community Struggles
by Marcos Inhauser 0-87178-238-3   8383

In the Beginning
by Wallace Ryan Kuroiwa 0-87178-415-7   8157

James: Faith in Action
by David S. Young 0-87178-456-4   8564

Jonah: God's Global Reach
by Paula Bowser 0-87178-474-2   8726

The Life of David
by Larry Fourman 0-87178-518-8   8188

The Lord's Prayer
by Mary Sue Rosenberger. 0-87178-541-2   8412

Love and Justice
by Eva O'Diam 0-87178-543-9   8439

Many Cultures, One in Christ
edited by Julie Garber 0-87178-547-1   8471

Mystery and Glory in John's Gospel
by Dorotha Winger Fry 0-87178-597-8   8978

Psalms
by John David Bowman 0-87178-723-7   8237

Presence and Power
by Robert W. Dell 0-87178-720-2   8202

Revelation
by Richard H. Lowery. 0-87178-739-3   8393

Sermon on the Mount
by Robert D. Bowman. 0-87178-777-6   8776